The Milky Way

by Gregory L. Vogt

Consultant:
Ralph Winrich
Former NASA Aerospace Education Specialist

Bridgestone Books
an imprint of Capstone Press
Mankato, Minnesota

Bridgestone Books are published by Capstone Press
151 Good Counsel Drive, P.O. Box 669, Mankato, Minnesota 56002
http://www.capstone-press.com

Library of Congress Cataloging-in-Publication Data
Vogt, Gregory.
    The Milky Way / by Gregory L. Vogt.
    p. cm.—(The galaxy)
    Includes bibliographical references and index.
    ISBN 0-7368-1384-5 (hardcover)
    1. Milky Way—Juvenile literature. [1. Milky Way. 2. Galaxies.] I. Title. II. Series.
QB857.7 .V64 2003
523.1′13—dc21   2001008153

Summary: Describes the objects that reside in the Milky Way galaxy, including stars,
    nebulas, clusters, and black holes, and explains what astronomers have discovered
    about other galaxies.

Editorial Credits
Tom Adamson, editor; Karen Risch, product planning editor; Timothy Halldin,
    series designer; Patrick Dentinger, book designer and illustrator; Kelly Garvin,
    photo researcher

Photo Credits
Bill Schoening/NOAO/AURA/NSF, 12
Gemini Observatory—GMOS Team, 6
The Hubble Heritage Team (STScI/AURA), 14
Jerry Schad, cover, 1, 4
NASA and Jeff Hester (Arizona State University), 13
NASA and Jeffrey Kenney and Elizabeth Yale (Yale University), 16
NASA and the Hubble Heritage Team (STScI/AURA), 20
NOAO/AURA/NSF, 18 (bottom)
Robert Williams and the Hubble Deep Field Team (STScI) and NASA, 18 (top)

1 2 3 4 5 6 07 06 05 04 03 02

Table of Contents

The Milky Way

In the summer night sky, people sometimes can see a faint band of light. This band of light is hard to see unless the sky is very dark. The band has wavy edges and dark areas. It looks like a river of milk flowing across the sky.

This milky band is called the Milky Way. It is a galaxy. Galaxies are collections of billions of stars. The Sun and all its planets belong to the Milky Way galaxy.

The Milky Way galaxy is shaped like a huge disk. Astronomers think the Milky Way galaxy is about 100,000 light-years across and 1,000 light-years thick. A light-year is a measurement for distances in space. It is the distance light travels in one year. One light-year is about 5.9 trillion miles (9.5 trillion kilometers).

On a very clear night, people sometimes can see a faint band of light in the sky called the Milky Way.

The Milky Way is like a giant spinning pinwheel. A large ball of stars called the nucleus is in the center. Five spiral arms come out from the nucleus. Each arm has a different name. The Sun is in the Orion arm. The Sun is about 30,000 light-years from the center of the galaxy.

All of the stars in the Milky Way galaxy are in constant motion. The stars move around the galaxy's nucleus. The Sun travels around the nucleus at a speed of about 138 miles (222 kilometers) per second.

In summer, the night sky faces toward the center of the Milky Way. In winter, the night sky faces away from the center. Fewer stars are in this direction. In winter, the Milky Way is harder to see.

Astronomers can only guess how many stars are in the Milky Way galaxy. They believe there are between 100 billion and 200 billion stars.

Astronomers think the Milky Way galaxy looks similar to this spiral galaxy.

Relative size of the Sun and the planets

The Sun's position in the solar system

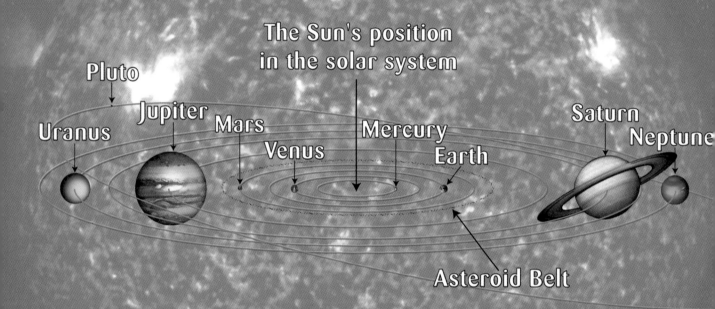

Pluto

Uranus

Jupiter

Mars

Venus

Mercury

Earth

Saturn

Neptune

Asteroid Belt

The Sun

The Sun is the closest star to Earth. Other stars in the Milky Way are very far away from Earth. Astronomers study the Sun to learn what other stars in the Milky Way are like.

The Sun is a giant ball of hot gases. It is made of the gases hydrogen and helium. Deep inside the Sun, hydrogen is heated and pressed together to form helium. Some of this hydrogen turns into energy that travels into space as light and heat. Every second, 4 million tons (3.6 million metric tons) of hydrogen turns into energy.

Planets and smaller objects travel around the Sun. Each planet is different. Jupiter, Saturn, Uranus, and Neptune are made of gas. Mercury, Venus, Earth, and Mars are made of rock. Pluto is made of ice and rock.

Astronomers think many other stars in the Milky Way also have planets. They have discovered large planets orbiting nearby stars.

◄ **This illustration compares the sizes of the planets and the Sun. The blue lines show the orbits of the planets. Thousands of asteroids move around the Sun. The asteroid belt is between the orbits of Mars and Jupiter.**

Betelgeuse

Earth
↓

Dwarf star
↓

The Sun

Sirius

Rigel

Stars in the Milky Way are different sizes, colors, and temperatures. The Sun is a yellow-white star. It is large enough to hold 1 million planets the size of Earth. The temperature of the Sun's surface is about 10,000 degrees Fahrenheit (5,500 degrees Celsius). The Sun's size and temperature make it an average star.

Some stars in the Milky Way are much larger than the Sun. The giant star Betelgeuse is about 600 times as large as the Sun. It is about as wide as Mars's orbit around the Sun. Betelgeuse is a red star about half as hot as the Sun. The star Rigel is blue-white and is about twice as hot as the Sun.

Other stars are much smaller than the Sun. The smallest stars in the galaxy are about the size of Earth. Some of these stars are white. White stars are very hot. Other stars are brown. Brown stars are called dwarfs. These stars are cooling off and will eventually become dark cinders.

Stars are different sizes and colors. Sirius is twice as big as the Sun. Other stars are much larger.

Nebulas

The dark areas in the Milky Way are actually clouds of dark gas and dust in space. These clouds are called nebulas. Some nebulas are in front of the Milky Way and block the milky glow.

Many nebulas are in the galaxy. These gas clouds are dark when they are far away from stars. Starlight reflects off nebulas when the nebulas are near stars. Nebulas can glow red, green, pink, yellow, and blue.

The Crab Nebula is a star that exploded in the year 1054.

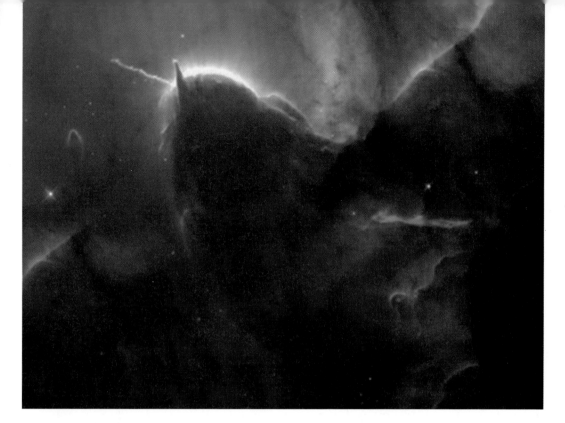

The Trifid Nebula is a star nursery. Stars are forming within this nebula.

Nebulas do different things. Some nebulas are leftovers after a star has exploded. Over time, people can see the gas cloud become larger. Other nebulas are star nurseries. The gas collects in large balls that in time become stars.

Clusters

The Milky Way is held together by gravity. Gravity is a force that attracts objects to each other. Gravity pulls some stars very close to each other. They orbit each other like the planets orbit the Sun. These stars are called double stars.

Gravity may bring many stars together. They look like swarms of fireflies. These groups of stars are called clusters.

Astronomers divide clusters into two types. Open clusters have a few hundred or a few thousand stars. The stars are about 1 or 2 light-years apart. Globular clusters are made up of thousands or millions of stars. These stars are jammed together. They are about one-tenth of a light-year apart.

This globular cluster has at least 100,000 stars. It is located about 28,000 light-years from Earth.

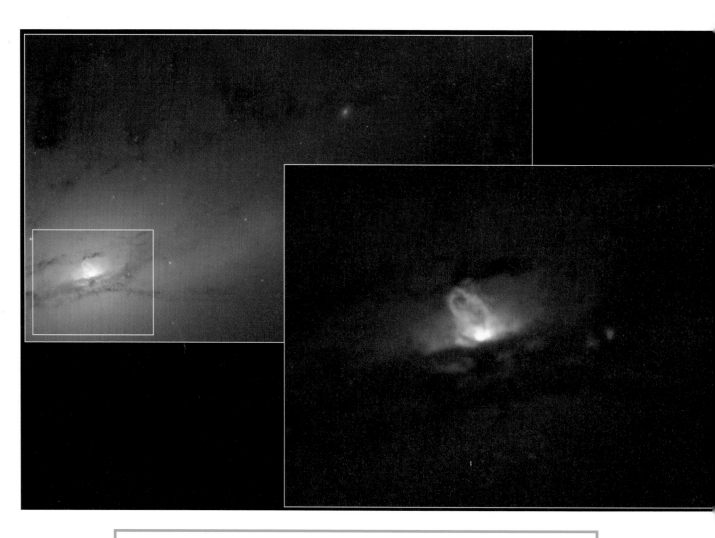

The image on the right is a close-up version of the photo on the left. The black hole itself cannot be seen. The photo shows material moving around the black hole. Matter gives off light as it gets drawn into the black hole.

Black Holes

Stars change when they run out of hydrogen fuel. Some stars become dark cinders. Others explode or just collapse.

Stars that collapse become very dense. The star's gravity pulls all the matter in the star tighter and tighter. Eventually, the star becomes very small. It seems to disappear.

Stars that collapse like this are called black holes. The matter in the star is still there. But the matter is squeezed together very tightly. It produces a powerful field of gravity. The gravity is so strong that anything that comes near the black hole will be sucked into it. Black holes even suck in light.

Black holes are like drainpipes in a galaxy. Anything that gets too close will be drawn in. Black holes will even suck in entire stars.

How Many Galaxies?

There are so many galaxies in the universe that astronomers cannot count them. They have estimated the number to be 100 billion or more. In one picture, astronomers counted 1,500 galaxies. The area of space covered in the picture is as small as the area covered by a grain of rice held at arm's length.

The Large Magellanic Cloud is a close neighbor to the Milky Way galaxy. It is about 179,000 light-years away.

Other Galaxies

The Milky Way is one of many galaxies in space. Each galaxy is home to billions of stars. Astronomers have found galaxies in all directions from the Milky Way. Some are spiral galaxies like the Milky Way. Other galaxies are round or egg-shaped.

Two nearby galaxies are called the Large and Small Magellanic Clouds. These galaxies are named after ocean explorer Ferdinand Magellan. South of Earth's equator, they are visible as fuzzy areas in the sky. These galaxies are small. Between them, they have only about 25 billion stars.

Some galaxies have an unusual spiral shape. This type of galaxy is called a barred spiral. A bar-shaped line of stars runs through the nucleus. A spiral arm comes out of each end of the bar.

When Galaxies Collide

Astronomers see some surprising things when they look far into space. Some galaxies are moving toward each other. These are colliding galaxies.

The collisions are not like head-on car crashes. There are no loud bangs. Instead, the galaxies pass right through each other.

Each colliding galaxy is home to billions of stars. Their stars are very far apart. A few stars may hit, but most stars miss each other. But the collision changes the galaxies. Gravity from both galaxies rearranges some of the stars as they pass through.

If a very big galaxy and a small galaxy collide, the small galaxy is destroyed. Gravity from the big galaxy captures all the stars from the smaller one. The stars in the small galaxy join the big galaxy.

These two spiral galaxies are colliding. Astronomers think that the one on the left will eventually capture the one on the right to form one larger galaxy.

Hands On: Swirling Galaxies

You can make a model of a spiral galaxy. Watch how the model forms spiral arms.

What You Need

Large mixing bowl
Water
Wooden spoon
Blue food coloring

What You Do

1. Fill the mixing bowl with water up to about 1 inch (2.5 centimeters) from the top. Wait until the water is still.
2. Use the handle end of the wooden spoon to stir the water in the middle. Make tight circles until all the surface water in the bowl is moving.
3. Squeeze five drops of blue food coloring into the middle of the water.
4. Watch the food coloring form the shape of a galaxy. The food coloring represents billions of stars.

The water in the center of the bowl circles faster than the water at the edges. The food coloring stretches out in long spirals. Galaxies spin the same way. The stars at the center circle faster than the stars at the edge.

Words to Know

asteroid (ASS-tuh-roid)—a large space rock that orbits the Sun; asteroids are too small to be called planets.

astronomer (uh-STRON-uh-mer)—a person who studies planets, stars, and space

cluster (KLUHSS-tur)—a group of stars that are close together; a star cluster may contain 100 stars or more than 1 million stars.

collide (kuh-LIDE)—to crash together

galaxy (GAL-uhk-see)—a large group of billions of stars

gravity (GRAV-uh-tee)—a force that pulls objects together

light-year (LITE-yeer)—a unit for measuring distance in space; a light-year is the distance light travels in one year, about 5.9 trillion miles (9.5 trillion kilometers).

nebula (NEB-yuh-luh)—a cloud of gas and dust in space

nucleus (NOO-klee-uhss)—the center of a galaxy

Read More

Kerrod, Robin. *Galaxies.* Looking at Stars. North Mankato, Minn.: Thameside Press, 2001.

Vogt, Gregory. *The Milky Way and Other Galaxies.* Our Universe. Austin, Texas: Steadwell Books, 2001.

Useful Addresses

Canadian Space Agency
6767 Route de l'Aéroport
Saint-Hubert, QC J3Y 8Y9
Canada

Lowell Observatory
1400 West Mars Hill Road
Flagstaff, AZ 86001

NASA Headquarters
Washington, DC 20546-0001

Internet Sites

Astronomy Picture of the Day—Barred Spiral Galaxy
http://antwrp.gsfc.nasa.gov/apod/ap001004.html
StarChild: A Learning Center for Young Astronomers
http://starchild.gsfc.nasa.gov/docs/StarChild/StarChild.html

Index